Thank you for purchasing our book.
We hope you love it!

"In the fast-paced world of pharmaceutical sales, mastering the art of negotiation is crucial to achieving success. "Negotiation Mastery: Strategies for Pharmaceutical Sales Reps" is your ultimate guide to developing persuasive communication skills and closing deals with confidence.

Copyrights©

This content is copyright of
Maples Book Solutions© 2024.
All rights reserved.

Table Of Contents

Chapter 1: Introduction to Negotiation in Pharmaceutical Sales   3

Chapter 2: Mastering Negotiations with Healthcare Professionals   9

Chapter 3: Key Negotiation Techniques for Pharmaceutical Sales Reps   17

Chapter 4: Building Rapport with Healthcare Professionals   25

Chapter 5: Conflict Resolution Strategies in Pharma Sales   35

Chapter 6: Effective Communication Skills for Pharmaceutical Negotiations   43

Chapter 7: Understanding Doctor and Pharmacist Motivations   51

Chapter 8: Team Collaboration Strategies in Pharmaceutical Sales   61

Chapter 9: Data-Driven Negotiation Tactics for Pharma Reps   70

Chapter 10: Ethical Considerations in Pharmaceutical Negotiations   79

Chapter 11: Role-Playing Scenarios for Sales Training   87

Chapter 12: Leveraging Technology in Pharmaceutical Negotiations   96

Chapter 13: Conclusion and Next Steps   105

Chapter 1: Introduction to Negotiation in Pharmaceutical Sales

The Importance of Negotiation Skills

Negotiation skills are essential for pharmaceutical sales representatives, enabling them to successfully navigate the complexities of their interactions with healthcare professionals.

These skills facilitate effective communication and enhance the ability to build rapport with doctors, pharmacists, and even colleagues. In a field where relationships are pivotal, mastering negotiation can lead to mutual understanding and better outcomes for both sales representatives and their clients.

By honing these skills, sales reps can position themselves as trusted partners rather than mere vendors, fostering long-term professional relationships that benefit all parties.

Effective negotiation techniques empower pharmaceutical sales representatives to identify and understand the motivations of doctors and pharmacists.

Recognizing what drives healthcare professionals in their decision-making processes allows sales reps to tailor their pitches and proposals accordingly. This understanding can lead to more fruitful discussions, wherein sales representatives present their products as solutions to the specific needs and concerns of healthcare providers.

Moreover, these tailored approaches can significantly enhance the likelihood of closing deals, as they resonate more deeply with the client's priorities.

Conflict resolution strategies are another critical component of negotiation skills in pharmaceutical sales. In the competitive landscape of healthcare, disagreements may arise regarding pricing, product efficacy, or other concerns. Having the ability to navigate these conflicts calmly and constructively is crucial.

Sales representatives who are equipped to manage disputes effectively can turn potential obstacles into opportunities for collaboration, reinforcing their role as problem solvers. This not only preserves relationships but also builds credibility and trust among clients, paving the way for future negotiations.

Communication skills are at the heart of successful negotiations. Pharmaceutical sales representatives must be adept at articulating their value propositions clearly and persuasively. This involves not only providing information about products but also actively listening to feedback and concerns from healthcare professionals.

Engaging in two-way communication fosters a sense of partnership and understanding, which can significantly influence the negotiation process.

Additionally, leveraging technology can enhance communication efforts, allowing for more efficient exchanges of information and updates that keep all stakeholders informed and engaged.

Lastly, the ethical considerations surrounding pharmaceutical negotiations cannot be overlooked. Maintaining integrity and transparency is vital in building trust with healthcare professionals. Sales representatives must navigate the fine line between persuasive selling and ethical responsibility, ensuring that their negotiation tactics do not compromise their values or the trust of their clients.

By prioritizing ethical practices, pharmaceutical sales reps can create an environment of respect and professionalism, which ultimately leads to more successful negotiations and sustainable business relationships.

Overview of the Pharmaceutical Sales Landscape

The pharmaceutical sales landscape is characterized by a unique interplay of scientific knowledge, regulatory considerations, and interpersonal skills. Sales representatives operate in a highly competitive environment where understanding the nuances of both the product and the healthcare system is crucial.

The landscape is shaped by the rapid advancement of medical research, the evolution of healthcare policies, and an increasingly informed patient population.

As representatives navigate this terrain, they must master the art of negotiation not only to secure sales but also to build lasting relationships with healthcare professionals.

Understanding the motivations of doctors and pharmacists is essential for successful negotiations.

Healthcare professionals are often bombarded with information and sales pitches from multiple sources, making it crucial for pharmaceutical sales reps to differentiate themselves.

By comprehensively understanding the needs and concerns of these professionals, sales representatives can tailor their approaches to resonate with the specific preferences and priorities of their audience.

This requires active listening and the ability to ask insightful questions that reveal underlying motivations.

Building rapport with healthcare professionals is a foundational aspect of the pharmaceutical sales process. Trust is paramount in these relationships, and it is developed over time through consistent engagement and follow-through.

Effective communication skills are vital in this regard; representatives must convey complex medical information in an accessible manner while also remaining sensitive to the time constraints faced by doctors and pharmacists.

By fostering a collaborative dialogue, sales representatives can position themselves as valuable partners in the healthcare process rather than mere vendors.

Conflict resolution is another critical component of the pharmaceutical sales landscape. Disagreements may arise due to differing opinions on product efficacy, pricing, or ethical considerations.

In such instances, employing negotiation techniques that prioritize empathy and understanding can lead to more favorable outcomes.

Data-driven negotiation tactics can provide representatives with insights that inform their strategies, enabling them to present compelling arguments based on empirical evidence.

Additionally, the use of digital tools for communication and relationship management can streamline interactions with healthcare professionals, making it easier to maintain connections and follow up on leads.

As the landscape continues to evolve, pharmaceutical sales representatives must remain adaptable, continuously updating their skills and approaches to thrive in a dynamic market.

Chapter 2: Mastering Negotiations with Healthcare Professionals

Strategies for Engaging Doctors

Engaging doctors effectively requires a deep understanding of their motivations, challenges, and the healthcare environment in which they operate.

Pharmaceutical sales representatives must prioritize building rapport with healthcare professionals by demonstrating genuine interest in their practices and patient care. This connection goes beyond casual conversation; it involves active listening, empathy, and a willingness to address the specific needs of doctors. By investing time in understanding their workflow, preferences, and pain points, sales reps can position themselves as valuable partners rather than mere vendors.

Establishing credibility is crucial in negotiations with doctors. Sales representatives must come prepared with data that not only supports their product claims but also aligns with the clinical interests of the physicians. This includes presenting peer-reviewed studies, real-world evidence, and case studies that resonate with the doctor's specialty.

Integrating this information into discussions helps establish trust and positions the representative as a knowledgeable resource. Utilizing technology to streamline data presentation can further enhance engagement, making it easier for doctors to absorb and consider the information provided.

Another effective strategy for engaging doctors is to leverage the influence of key opinion leaders (KOLs) within the medical community. Collaborating with respected figures can lend credibility to the sales rep's message and enhance the perceived value of the product.

Organizing educational events or webinars featuring KOLs can facilitate discussions around the therapeutic area, fostering an environment where doctors feel more comfortable asking questions and expressing concerns. This approach not only enhances engagement but also positions the sales rep as a facilitator of knowledge rather than just a salesperson.

Conflict resolution strategies are also essential when navigating challenging discussions with healthcare professionals. Pharmaceuticals sales reps should be trained to recognize potential objections or resistance from doctors and respond with empathy and understanding.

By addressing concerns directly and providing clear, evidence-based responses, reps can turn objections into opportunities for deeper dialogue. This not only strengthens the relationship but also helps the doctor feel heard and valued, fostering long-term engagement.

Finally, effective communication skills are paramount in all interactions with doctors. Sales representatives should practice clear, concise, and respectful communication that respects the doctor's time and expertise.

Role-playing scenarios can be a useful training tool to hone these skills, allowing reps to simulate various negotiation situations and refine their approaches.

Additionally, being adaptable in communication style to suit the preferences of individual doctors can make a significant difference in engagement levels.

By combining these strategies, pharmaceutical sales representatives can enhance their negotiation outcomes and build lasting partnerships with healthcare professionals.

Approaching Pharmacists Effectively

Approaching pharmacists effectively requires a nuanced understanding of their unique role within the healthcare ecosystem. Pharmacists are not only dispensers of medication but also critical healthcare providers who play a significant role in patient outcomes.

Sales representatives must recognize the importance of building a solid relationship with pharmacists, as their insights and recommendations can greatly influence prescribing behaviors and patient adherence to therapy.

Emphasizing this collaborative approach fosters an environment where both pharmacists and sales reps can work towards common goals, ultimately enhancing patient care.

To engage pharmacists successfully, sales representatives should prioritize active listening and effective communication. It is essential to approach each interaction with an open mind, ready to understand the pharmacist's perspective and challenges.

By asking open-ended questions and demonstrating a genuine interest in their day-to-day experiences, reps can uncover valuable insights that can inform their sales strategies. This rapport-building technique not only establishes trust but also positions the sales rep as a supportive partner rather than merely a vendor.

Data-driven negotiation tactics play a crucial role in discussions with pharmacists. Sales reps should come prepared with relevant data that highlights the benefits of their products, including efficacy, safety, and cost-effectiveness.

Tailoring this information to address specific concerns or interests of the pharmacist can significantly enhance the effectiveness of the conversation. Additionally, being knowledgeable about current industry trends and regulatory changes can further establish credibility and demonstrate the rep's commitment to providing value to the pharmacist's practice.

Understanding the motivations of pharmacists is essential for effective negotiation. Pharmacists are often driven by a desire to ensure patient safety, optimize therapeutic outcomes, and manage their workload efficiently. By aligning sales presentations with these motivations, reps can create compelling arguments that resonate with pharmacists' values. For instance, showcasing how a product can streamline their workflow or improve patient adherence can lead to more productive discussions and a greater likelihood of securing support for the product.

Finally, ethical considerations should always underpin interactions with pharmacists. Transparency and honesty are paramount in building long-lasting relationships based on mutual respect. Sales representatives must be mindful of the ethical implications of their negotiations and strive to foster an environment of collaboration rather than competition. By prioritizing the well-being of patients and upholding professional standards, pharmaceutical sales reps can cultivate trust with pharmacists that not only enhances individual negotiations but also contributes to a positive reputation for their organization within the healthcare community.

Building Relationships with Healthcare Teams

Building strong relationships with healthcare teams is essential for pharmaceutical sales representatives seeking to excel in their roles. These teams, which often include doctors, pharmacists, and various healthcare professionals, play a pivotal role in the decision-making process regarding medication choices. Establishing rapport with these individuals can lead to more effective negotiations and ultimately improve patient care outcomes. Understanding the dynamics of these relationships is key to achieving success in pharmaceutical sales.

To build effective relationships, it is crucial to approach healthcare professionals with genuine respect and empathy. Sales representatives should take the time to understand the unique challenges faced by doctors and pharmacists, such as time constraints, regulatory pressures, and patient needs. By demonstrating a willingness to listen and engage in meaningful conversations, sales reps can foster a sense of trust and collaboration. This rapport not only enhances communication but also encourages healthcare teams to be more receptive to discussing products and solutions that align with their objectives.

Effective communication skills are fundamental in establishing and maintaining these relationships. Sales representatives must be adept at articulating their value propositions while being sensitive to the specific interests and motivations of healthcare professionals. Tailoring messages to address the concerns of doctors and pharmacists can significantly enhance the effectiveness of negotiations. Moreover, utilizing active listening techniques ensures that reps are fully attuned to the needs and feedback of healthcare teams, which can help in adjusting strategies in real-time.

Conflict resolution is another critical aspect of relationship-building within healthcare teams. Disagreements may arise due to differing priorities or misunderstandings about product benefits. Sales representatives should be equipped with strategies to address conflicts constructively, focusing on finding common ground and shared goals. By demonstrating a commitment to resolving issues amicably and collaboratively, reps can reinforce their credibility and strengthen their relationships with healthcare professionals.

Lastly, leveraging technology can enhance relationship-building efforts with healthcare teams. Utilizing customer relationship management (CRM) systems and data analytics can provide valuable insights into the preferences and behaviors of healthcare professionals. This data-driven approach enables sales representatives to tailor their interactions and follow-ups more effectively, ensuring that they remain relevant and engaged. By combining technological tools with interpersonal skills, pharmaceutical sales reps can create a holistic strategy that nurtures long-lasting relationships within healthcare teams, ultimately leading to more successful negotiations and improved outcomes for all parties involved.

Chapter 3: Key Negotiation Techniques for Pharmaceutical Sales Reps

The Art of Persuasion

The art of persuasion is a critical skill for pharmaceutical sales representatives, as it directly influences the success of negotiations with healthcare professionals. Understanding the motivations and needs of doctors and pharmacists is essential in crafting persuasive messages that resonate with their interests. By emphasizing the benefits of a product in the context of patient care, sales reps can create a compelling narrative that aligns the pharmaceutical offering with the healthcare provider's goals. This approach not only fosters trust but also enhances the likelihood of a favorable outcome during negotiations.

Building rapport with healthcare professionals is a foundational element of effective persuasion. Establishing a genuine connection allows sales representatives to engage in open dialogue, making it easier to identify the specific concerns or objections the healthcare professional may have. Utilizing active listening techniques and demonstrating empathy can significantly strengthen this rapport.

When healthcare providers feel understood and valued, they are more inclined to consider the proposals presented, facilitating a smoother negotiation process.

Conflict resolution strategies play a crucial role in the persuasive negotiation landscape. It is inevitable that disagreements or misunderstandings will arise during discussions. Being prepared to address these conflicts constructively can turn potential roadblocks into opportunities for further engagement. By employing techniques such as reframing the conversation, identifying common ground, and seeking collaborative solutions, pharmaceutical sales reps can navigate challenges effectively, reinforcing their persuasive efforts while maintaining positive relationships with healthcare professionals.

Effective communication skills are paramount in the art of persuasion. Clarity of message, confidence in delivery, and the ability to adapt one's communication style to different audiences are key components of successful negotiations. Sales reps should focus on articulating their value propositions in a way that is not only informative but also engaging. Visual aids, data-driven insights, and real-world examples can enhance the persuasive impact of their presentations. Additionally, being aware of non-verbal cues can help sales reps adjust their approach in real time, ensuring that they remain aligned with the healthcare professional's responses.

Incorporating ethical considerations into the art of persuasion is vital in the pharmaceutical industry. Sales representatives must navigate a complex landscape where compliance and integrity are paramount. By prioritizing ethical practices, such as transparency and respect for the healthcare professional's autonomy, sales reps can build a foundation of trust that strengthens their persuasive efforts. In doing so, they not only enhance their credibility but also contribute to a more positive perception of the pharmaceutical industry as a whole, fostering long-term relationships that benefit all parties involved.

Active Listening Skills

Active listening is a crucial skill for pharmaceutical sales representatives, serving as the foundation for effective communication and successful negotiations with healthcare professionals. This skill goes beyond simply hearing the words being spoken; it involves fully engaging with the speaker, understanding their message, and responding thoughtfully. In the fast-paced world of pharmaceuticals, where the stakes are high and relationships matter, mastering active listening can significantly enhance your ability to connect with doctors, pharmacists, and coworkers, ultimately driving successful outcomes.

To develop active listening skills, it is essential to cultivate an awareness of both verbal and non-verbal cues. This includes paying attention to tone, pace, and body language, which can provide valuable context to the spoken words. As you engage with healthcare professionals, observe their reactions and adjust your approach accordingly. This attentiveness not only demonstrates respect but also helps to build rapport, fostering a trusting environment that can lead to more fruitful negotiations.

By showing that you value their input and perspectives, you encourage open dialogue, which is vital in understanding their motivations and concerns.

Another key aspect of active listening is the practice of paraphrasing and summarizing what the speaker has communicated. This technique serves multiple purposes; it confirms your understanding of their message and allows the speaker to clarify any misunderstandings. In the context of pharmaceutical sales, where complex information may be discussed, summarizing key points helps ensure that both parties are aligned. This practice not only reinforces the relationship but also positions you as a knowledgeable partner who is committed to addressing the needs of healthcare professionals.

Moreover, effective questioning techniques play a significant role in active listening. Open-ended questions encourage deeper discussion and allow healthcare professionals to express their thoughts and feelings more freely. In negotiations, these questions can uncover underlying motivations, enabling you to tailor your proposals to meet their specific needs.

By fostering an environment where healthcare professionals feel comfortable sharing their insights, you create opportunities for collaboration, leading to mutually beneficial outcomes.

Lastly, developing active listening skills requires ongoing practice and self-reflection. Consider role-playing scenarios with colleagues to simulate negotiations and enhance your listening techniques. Additionally, seek feedback from teammates and mentors, as their perspectives can provide valuable insights into your listening habits. By continuously honing your active listening skills, you will not only improve your negotiation abilities but also strengthen your professional relationships within the pharmaceutical industry, ultimately contributing to your long-term success.

Tailoring Your Approach

Tailoring your approach in pharmaceutical negotiations is essential for maximizing your effectiveness as a sales representative. Each interaction with healthcare professionals—be it doctors, pharmacists, or colleagues—requires a nuanced understanding of their unique motivations and concerns. By customizing your strategy to align with their perspectives, you can foster stronger relationships and enhance the likelihood of a successful outcome. This subchapter will explore key strategies for tailoring your negotiation approach, emphasizing the importance of preparation, active listening, and adaptability.

Preparation is the cornerstone of any successful negotiation. Prior to your meetings, invest time in researching the individual you are engaging with, their practice, and the specific challenges they face. Understanding their patient demographics, treatment philosophies, and any recent changes in healthcare regulations can provide you with critical insights. Additionally, familiarize yourself with your product's features and benefits in the context of their needs. This foundational knowledge will allow you to present your offerings in a way that resonates with the healthcare professional's priorities, thereby enhancing your credibility and rapport.

Active listening is another crucial component of tailoring your approach. During negotiations, it's vital to engage fully with what the other party is saying, rather than merely waiting for your turn to speak. By demonstrating genuine interest in their viewpoints, you can uncover underlying motivations and concerns that may not be immediately apparent. This practice not only helps you address their needs more effectively but also shows that you value their input. Establishing this two-way communication fosters a collaborative environment, making it easier to navigate potential conflicts and reach mutually beneficial agreements.

Flexibility and adaptability in your negotiation tactics are equally important. Each negotiation scenario is unique, and what works well in one situation may not be effective in another. Be prepared to pivot your approach based on the dynamics of the conversation. For instance, if a doctor expresses skepticism about your product, consider shifting from a data-heavy presentation to a more narrative-driven discussion that highlights patient success stories. This adaptability will help you maintain engagement and build trust, as it demonstrates your commitment to addressing their specific concerns.

Finally, leveraging technology can significantly enhance your negotiation strategy. Utilize data-driven tools and software that can provide real-time insights into market trends, competitor activities, and customer preferences. By backing your proposals with solid data, you can reinforce your arguments and instill confidence in healthcare professionals. Moreover, technology can facilitate seamless communication and collaboration among your team members, ensuring that everyone is aligned and informed. By embracing these technological advancements, you can further refine your tailored approach and improve your overall negotiation outcomes in the pharmaceutical landscape.

Chapter 4: Building Rapport with Healthcare Professionals

Establishing Trust

Establishing trust is a cornerstone of successful negotiations in pharmaceutical sales. Trust between pharmaceutical sales representatives and healthcare professionals is essential for fostering long-term relationships that can lead to successful outcomes. When doctors and pharmacists feel confident in your integrity and expertise, they are more likely to engage openly and consider your proposals seriously. Building this trust requires a strategic approach that incorporates understanding the motivations of healthcare professionals, demonstrating credibility, and maintaining consistent communication.

To establish trust, it is crucial to understand the underlying motivations of doctors and pharmacists. Each healthcare professional brings unique perspectives and priorities to the table. Some may prioritize patient outcomes, while others might focus on cost-effectiveness or the latest clinical data. By actively listening to their concerns and demonstrating that you understand their priorities, you can tailor your approach to meet their needs. This understanding not only shows respect for their expertise but also positions you as a partner rather than just a vendor.

Credibility is another vital component of trust. To build credibility, pharmaceutical sales representatives must be well-versed in the products they represent, as well as the latest developments in the pharmaceutical industry and relevant clinical research. Being able to provide accurate, reliable information and answer questions confidently reinforces your role as a knowledgeable resource. Additionally, sharing testimonials or case studies from other healthcare professionals can enhance your credibility further, as it provides concrete examples of your product's value and effectiveness.

Effective communication skills play a significant role in establishing trust. Transparency is key; being open about the limitations of your products, as well as potential conflicts of interest, fosters an environment where healthcare professionals feel comfortable discussing their reservations. Moreover, utilizing active listening techniques helps to validate their concerns and demonstrates genuine interest in their needs. When healthcare professionals perceive that you value their opinions, they are more likely to reciprocate that trust.

Lastly, ongoing relationship management is essential for maintaining trust. Following up after initial meetings, providing updates on new product information, and checking in on how your solutions are performing for them are all strategies that reinforce your commitment to their success. Additionally, collaborating with your coworkers to ensure consistent messaging and support can enhance trust not only with healthcare professionals but also within your team. By prioritizing trust-building strategies, pharmaceutical sales representatives can create a solid foundation for successful negotiations that benefit both parties involved.

The Role of Empathy in Negotiations

Empathy is a crucial component in negotiations, especially in the pharmaceutical sales environment. When sales representatives approach healthcare professionals, understanding their perspectives and emotions can significantly impact the outcome of discussions. Empathy allows reps to connect with doctors and pharmacists on a human level, fostering trust and rapport. This emotional intelligence not only facilitates a more open dialogue but also enables sales reps to tailor their pitches to meet the specific needs and concerns of their audience. By actively listening and demonstrating genuine care for the healthcare professionals' challenges, sales reps can create an environment conducive to collaborative problem-solving.

In the context of pharmaceutical sales, healthcare professionals often face numerous pressures, including time constraints, patient care responsibilities, and staying updated with the latest medical advancements. By employing empathy, sales reps can better understand these pressures and position their products as solutions that alleviate some of these burdens.

This understanding allows reps to frame their negotiations in a way that highlights mutual benefits, thereby increasing the likelihood of a positive outcome. Moreover, when healthcare providers sense that their needs are being prioritized, they are more likely to engage in an open and constructive negotiation process.

Building rapport through empathy is also essential in long-term relationship management. The pharmaceutical industry thrives on relationships, and a strong bond with healthcare professionals can lead to repeat business and referrals. By consistently demonstrating empathy, sales reps can establish themselves as trusted partners rather than mere vendors.

This shift in perception can be pivotal, as healthcare professionals are more inclined to consider recommendations from those they feel genuinely understand their circumstances and motivations. When negotiations become more collaborative, it often results in outcomes that satisfy both parties and contribute to a healthier professional relationship.

Conflict is inevitable in negotiations, but empathy can be a powerful tool for resolution. When tensions arise, whether due to differences in priorities or misunderstandings, an empathetic approach helps de-escalate the situation. By acknowledging the other party's feelings and viewpoints, sales reps can create a safe space for open communication. This approach not only addresses the immediate conflict but also reinforces the relationship, as it showcases the rep's commitment to finding a win-win solution. Emphasizing common goals and understanding the underlying motivations can turn potential confrontations into opportunities for deeper collaboration.

Finally, effective communication skills are enhanced through empathy. When sales reps can articulate their message while being sensitive to the emotions and concerns of their audience, they are more likely to achieve favorable results. Empathy enriches the negotiation process by encouraging clarity, active listening, and appropriate responses. It allows reps to adapt their communication styles to match the preferences of healthcare professionals, thereby fostering a more engaging and productive dialogue. In the competitive landscape of pharmaceutical sales, mastering the role of empathy in negotiations can be a defining factor that sets successful representatives apart from their peers.

Networkingstrategien

Networking is a crucial component of success in pharmaceutical sales, as it facilitates the establishment of strong relationships with healthcare professionals, colleagues, and industry stakeholders. One effective strategy is to identify and engage with key opinion leaders (KOLs) within the medical community. KOLs are influential figures whose insights can significantly impact the perceptions and acceptance of products.

By attending conferences, participating in medical seminars, or collaborating on research projects, pharmaceutical sales representatives can foster connections with these individuals. This not only enhances their credibility but also provides valuable opportunities to learn more about the needs and motivations of healthcare professionals, which can inform negotiation strategies.

Another important aspect of networking is leveraging existing relationships to expand your professional network. Sales representatives should actively seek referrals and introductions from doctors, pharmacists, and colleagues. A warm introduction can often lead to more productive conversations than a cold outreach, as trust and rapport are already established. Engaging in regular follow-ups with contacts can help maintain these relationships, ensuring that sales representatives remain top-of-mind when healthcare professionals require new solutions or products. This approach emphasizes the importance of nurturing relationships over time, rather than solely focusing on immediate sales outcomes.

Utilizing technology can significantly enhance networking efforts in the pharmaceutical industry. Social media platforms, especially LinkedIn, provide an avenue for sales representatives to connect with healthcare professionals, share industry insights, and participate in discussions relevant to their field. Participating in online forums and professional groups can also facilitate knowledge exchange and establish the representative as a credible source of information.

Additionally, CRM (Customer Relationship Management) systems can be instrumental in tracking interactions and managing relationships, ensuring that no opportunity for engagement is overlooked.

Building rapport with healthcare professionals is essential for successful negotiations. Sales representatives should focus on understanding the unique challenges faced by doctors and pharmacists, as well as their motivations and goals.

Active listening and empathy are vital skills in this regard, allowing representatives to tailor their approaches to meet the specific needs of their contacts. Engaging in meaningful conversations that go beyond product features can help establish a strong foundation of trust, making it easier to negotiate effectively when the time comes.

Finally, networking should also encompass collaboration with coworkers and team members. A cohesive team can share valuable insights and strategies that can enhance individual performance. Regular team meetings that encourage sharing of experiences and challenges faced in the field can foster a supportive environment.

Role-playing scenarios can also be utilized to practice negotiation techniques and conflict resolution strategies, ensuring that all team members are equipped to represent the company effectively. By cultivating a culture of collaboration and collective problem-solving, pharmaceutical sales representatives can enhance their networking capabilities and overall success in negotiations.

Chapter 5: Conflict Resolution Strategies in Pharma Sales

Identifying Sources of Conflict

Identifying sources of conflict is a crucial step for pharmaceutical sales representatives aiming to enhance their negotiation skills. Conflicts can arise from various factors, including differing objectives, miscommunication, and the pressure of meeting sales targets. For sales reps, understanding the underlying causes of conflict with healthcare professionals, such as doctors and pharmacists, can lead to more effective negotiation strategies. By recognizing these sources, representatives can tailor their approaches to foster collaboration instead of confrontation, ultimately leading to better outcomes for all parties involved.

One primary source of conflict in pharmaceutical sales stems from the differing priorities of sales reps and healthcare professionals. While sales representatives are typically focused on meeting sales quotas and promoting their products, doctors and pharmacists prioritize patient care and outcomes. This divergence can create tension, particularly when a sales rep feels that a healthcare professional is dismissing their product without fully considering its benefits. Identifying this conflict requires sales representatives to empathize with healthcare professionals' perspectives, understanding their motivations and constraints.

Miscommunication is another significant source of conflict in pharmaceutical negotiations. Ambiguities in messaging, whether in the form of product information or expectations regarding the sales process, can lead to misunderstandings. For instance, if a sales representative fails to clarify the limitations of a drug's efficacy or potential side effects, a healthcare professional may feel misled, resulting in distrust and conflict. To mitigate this risk, sales reps should prioritize clear and transparent communication, ensuring that all parties have a mutual understanding of the information being presented.

Additionally, external pressures, such as market competition and regulatory changes, can exacerbate conflicts in the pharmaceutical sales environment. Representatives may feel compelled to push their products aggressively, while healthcare professionals may be grappling with their own pressures from patients, insurance companies, and regulatory bodies. Recognizing these external factors can help sales reps adopt a more collaborative approach, focusing on how their products can genuinely assist healthcare professionals in meeting their own goals rather than simply pushing for a sale.

Lastly, the dynamics within a sales team can also be a source of conflict that affects negotiations with external stakeholders. Competition among team members for recognition and resources can lead to a lack of support and communication, hindering overall effectiveness. Sales reps must cultivate a culture of teamwork and open communication within their teams, sharing insights and strategies that can enhance everyone's performance. By addressing internal conflicts and fostering collaboration, sales representatives can better position themselves to navigate external negotiations with healthcare professionals, ultimately leading to more successful outcomes.

Techniques for Resolving Disputes

Disputes in the pharmaceutical sales environment can arise from various sources, including misunderstandings between sales representatives and healthcare professionals, conflicting priorities among team members, or challenges in achieving consensus on sales strategies. To effectively resolve these disputes, sales representatives must rely on a combination of communication skills, emotional intelligence, and strategic thinking. A structured approach to conflict resolution not only helps in addressing the immediate issues but also strengthens relationships and builds trust with doctors, pharmacists, and colleagues.

One effective technique for resolving disputes is active listening. This involves genuinely engaging with the other party's perspective and demonstrating empathy towards their concerns. By asking open-ended questions and paraphrasing their statements, pharmaceutical sales representatives can clarify misunderstandings and identify the root cause of the conflict. This technique encourages open dialogue and signals to the other party that their opinions are valued, which can ultimately lead to a more collaborative problem-solving process.

Another important strategy is to focus on interests rather than positions. In negotiations, parties often become entrenched in their positions, leading to a zero-sum mentality that can escalate conflicts. By shifting the conversation to underlying interests—such as the healthcare provider's desire for patient outcomes or the sales rep's need for product visibility—both parties can explore mutually beneficial solutions. This approach fosters creativity in finding compromises and ensures that all stakeholders feel their essential needs are being addressed.

In addition to these techniques, employing a collaborative approach to conflict resolution can significantly enhance outcomes. This involves working together with the other party to brainstorm solutions and involving them in the decision-making process. By creating a sense of ownership and shared responsibility, sales representatives can transform adversarial situations into opportunities for partnership. This not only resolves the immediate dispute but also lays the groundwork for future collaboration and effective teamwork, which are crucial in the competitive pharmaceutical landscape.

Lastly, it is essential to remain mindful of ethical considerations throughout the negotiation process. Maintaining transparency and integrity builds credibility and trust with healthcare professionals and colleagues alike. By adhering to ethical standards, pharmaceutical sales representatives can navigate disputes in a manner that reinforces their reputation and fosters long-term relationships. Ultimately, these techniques for resolving disputes are not simply about overcoming obstacles; they are integral to mastering negotiations and achieving success in the pharmaceutical sales arena.

Turning Conflict into Opportunity

Turning conflict into opportunity is a crucial skill for pharmaceutical sales representatives navigating the complexities of their field. Conflicts can arise in various situations, whether during negotiations with healthcare professionals, internal team discussions, or while addressing customer concerns. Recognizing that conflict is not inherently negative but rather a potential catalyst for growth is essential. By approaching conflict with a mindset focused on collaboration and problem-solving, sales representatives can transform challenging situations into valuable opportunities that enhance relationships and drive sales success.

To effectively turn conflict into opportunity, it is vital first to identify the underlying interests of all parties involved. In pharmaceutical sales, understanding the motivations of doctors, pharmacists, and team members is key to addressing their concerns and finding common ground. Sales representatives should actively listen and ask open-ended questions to uncover these interests. By demonstrating genuine curiosity and empathy, you can build rapport and create a safe environment for dialogue. This approach not only mitigates tension but also fosters trust, making it easier to navigate through conflicts productively.

Once the interests are clear, representatives should focus on collaborative problem-solving. This involves brainstorming solutions that satisfy the needs of all parties involved. Encouraging input from healthcare professionals can lead to innovative ideas that benefit both the sales representative and the client. For instance, if a doctor expresses hesitation about prescribing a certain medication, discussing their concerns and offering tailored data that addresses those issues can change the dynamics of the conversation. By positioning yourself as a partner rather than a mere vendor, you can turn a conflict into an opportunity for deeper engagement and enhanced credibility.

Effective communication skills play a pivotal role in transforming conflict into opportunity. Sales representatives must be adept at articulating their perspectives while remaining open to feedback. Utilizing techniques such as mirroring, paraphrasing, and summarizing can help clarify misunderstandings and reinforce that all viewpoints are valued. Furthermore, maintaining a calm and professional demeanor during conflicts can significantly influence the outcome. When representatives model effective communication, they set a standard for others involved in the negotiation, creating a collaborative atmosphere that encourages resolution.

Finally, leveraging technology and data-driven tactics can further enhance the potential for turning conflict into opportunity. Utilizing CRM systems and data analysis tools can provide insights into customer behavior and preferences, allowing representatives to tailor their approaches accordingly. In addition, role-playing scenarios can be implemented in team settings to prepare for potential conflicts, helping to refine negotiation strategies and improve team cohesion. By embracing these methods, pharmaceutical sales representatives not only resolve conflicts more effectively but also capitalize on them to strengthen relationships and drive sales outcomes.

Chapter 6: Effective Communication Skills for Pharmaceutical Negotiations

Verbal and Non-Verbal Communication

Verbal and non-verbal communication are fundamental components of successful negotiations in pharmaceutical sales. Verbal communication encompasses the words we choose and how we articulate them. In interactions with healthcare professionals, such as doctors and pharmacists, clarity and professionalism in language can significantly influence the outcome of negotiations. Using industry-specific terminology appropriately while ensuring that the message remains accessible is essential. Tailoring your vocabulary to match the knowledge level of your audience fosters mutual understanding and demonstrates respect for their expertise.

Non-verbal communication, including body language, facial expressions, and eye contact, plays a crucial role in conveying confidence and building rapport. During face-to-face meetings, a firm handshake, an open posture, and maintaining appropriate eye contact can signal your commitment and professionalism. Conversely, closed body language or lack of engagement can create barriers to effective communication. Pharmaceutical sales representatives must be mindful of their non-verbal signals, as these can often communicate more than spoken words. Developing awareness of one's own body language, as well as that of others, enables sales reps to adjust their approach dynamically during negotiations.

Active listening is another critical element that intertwines both verbal and non-verbal communication. It is essential for pharmaceutical sales representatives to not only express their points clearly but also to demonstrate genuine interest in the perspectives of healthcare professionals. This involves not only hearing what is said but also interpreting the underlying emotions and motivations. Techniques such as paraphrasing, summarizing, and asking open-ended questions can enhance understanding and show respect for the speaker's viewpoints, fostering a collaborative atmosphere.

Understanding the motivations and concerns of doctors and pharmacists can guide the negotiation process. By leveraging verbal communication to address specific needs and challenges faced by healthcare professionals, sales reps can position their products more effectively. Additionally, recognizing non-verbal cues that indicate interest or hesitation can provide valuable insights into the other party's mindset. This dual focus allows sales representatives to tailor their strategies in real-time, making adjustments that resonate with the audience's priorities.

Finally, fostering an environment of trust and collaboration is paramount in negotiations. Ethical considerations must underpin all communication strategies, ensuring that interactions are transparent and respectful. Building rapport with healthcare professionals involves consistent, honest communication that acknowledges their expertise and decision-making authority. By mastering both verbal and non-verbal communication techniques, pharmaceutical sales representatives can enhance their negotiation skills, leading to more successful outcomes in their interactions with doctors, pharmacists, and colleagues alike.

Crafting Your Message

Crafting your message is a critical component in the negotiation process for pharmaceutical sales representatives. The ability to convey your value proposition clearly and persuasively can significantly influence the outcome of your negotiations with healthcare professionals. To achieve this, it is essential to understand your audience, whether they are doctors, pharmacists, or your colleagues. Each group has unique motivations and concerns that must be addressed in your communication. Tailoring your message to resonate with these motivations will help you build rapport and establish trust.

Effective communication begins with clarity and conciseness. When presenting your products or solutions, avoid jargon and overly technical language that may alienate your audience. Instead, focus on the benefits your product offers, backed by data and real-world examples that demonstrate its effectiveness. Use storytelling techniques to illustrate how your product has positively impacted patients or improved healthcare outcomes. This approach not only engages your audience but also makes your message more relatable and memorable.

In addition to clarity, emotional intelligence plays a vital role in crafting your message. Understanding the emotional drivers of your audience allows you to connect on a deeper level. For instance, doctors may be motivated by patient outcomes, while pharmacists might prioritize efficiency and cost-effectiveness. Recognizing these motivations enables you to tailor your message accordingly, addressing their specific concerns and demonstrating how your product aligns with their goals. This connection fosters a collaborative atmosphere, making negotiations smoother and more productive.

Conflict resolution strategies are also essential in the negotiation process. Anticipating objections or concerns from healthcare professionals can help you prepare a thoughtful response. By addressing potential issues proactively in your messaging, you can alleviate doubts and reinforce the value of your offering. Role-playing scenarios can be an effective training tool for sales teams, allowing members to practice handling objections and refining their messaging in a safe environment. This preparation not only builds confidence but also enhances team collaboration, ensuring that everyone is on the same page during negotiations.

Finally, leveraging technology can significantly enhance how you craft and deliver your message. Digital tools can provide valuable insights into the preferences and behavior of your audience, enabling you to personalize your communications further. Utilizing data-driven tactics allows you to present compelling arguments supported by evidence, increasing your credibility. Additionally, tools such as virtual presentations or interactive demos can make your message more engaging and impactful. By integrating technology into your communication strategy, you can elevate your negotiation skills and achieve greater success in the competitive landscape of pharmaceutical sales.

Overcoming Communication Barriers

Overcoming communication barriers is essential for pharmaceutical sales representatives striving to achieve success in negotiations with healthcare professionals. Effective communication is not merely about exchanging information; it involves understanding the unique perspectives and motivations of doctors, pharmacists, and colleagues. Misunderstandings can arise from different terminologies, varying levels of knowledge about products, and distinct communication styles. Identifying these barriers is the first step in fostering productive dialogues that lead to successful negotiations.

One significant barrier in pharmaceutical sales is the specialized language often used within the industry. Technical jargon can alienate healthcare professionals who may not be familiar with specific terms, leading to confusion and disengagement. To mitigate this, sales representatives should strive to simplify their language and clarify any complex concepts. This approach not only helps in making the communication more accessible but also demonstrates respect for the expertise of the healthcare professionals. Adapting your language to the audience can enhance rapport and facilitate a more open exchange of ideas.

Cultural differences also play a crucial role in communication barriers. Each healthcare professional may come from a diverse background, influencing their communication preferences and negotiation styles. Understanding these cultural nuances can be instrumental in tailoring your approach. For instance, some cultures prioritize directness, while others may value a more indirect style of communication. Sales representatives should take the time to research and recognize these differences, ensuring that their communication is respectful and effective across a variety of cultural contexts.

Listening is a vital component of overcoming communication barriers. Active listening helps representatives identify the underlying concerns and motivations of doctors and pharmacists. By demonstrating genuine interest in what they are saying, sales representatives can build trust and encourage open dialogue. This practice not only reveals critical information that can guide negotiation strategies but also creates a collaborative atmosphere where both parties feel valued and understood. Listening attentively can transform potential conflicts into opportunities for mutual benefit.

Leveraging technology can also assist in overcoming communication barriers. Tools such as customer relationship management (CRM) systems, video conferencing, and instant messaging platforms can enhance communication efficiency and clarity. These technologies enable sales representatives to share information quickly, provide visual aids, and maintain a consistent flow of communication with their teams and clients. By integrating these tools into daily practices, pharmaceutical sales representatives can streamline their negotiations, ensuring that communication remains clear and effective throughout the sales process.

Chapter 7: Understanding Doctor and Pharmacist Motivations

Key Motivators for Healthcare Professionals

Understanding the key motivators for healthcare professionals is essential for pharmaceutical sales representatives aiming to enhance their negotiation skills. Healthcare professionals, including doctors and pharmacists, are driven by a variety of factors that influence their decisions and responses during negotiations. Recognizing these motivators allows sales reps to tailor their approach, build stronger relationships, and ultimately achieve better outcomes. The motivations can be categorized into intrinsic factors, such as personal values and professional fulfillment, and extrinsic factors, including financial incentives and career advancement opportunities.

One significant intrinsic motivator for healthcare professionals is their commitment to patient care. Most doctors and pharmacists enter their fields with a strong desire to help patients achieve better health outcomes. This dedication influences their decision-making process, as they prioritize treatments and solutions that are beneficial for their patients. Pharmaceutical sales representatives can connect with this motivation by emphasizing how their products improve patient care, supporting healthcare professionals in making informed decisions that align with their values.

Extrinsic motivators also play a crucial role in healthcare professionals' decisions. Financial incentives, including compensation and bonuses tied to patient outcomes or sales targets, can significantly influence their choices. Additionally, opportunities for professional development and career advancement are critical, as healthcare professionals often seek roles that allow them to grow their expertise and influence within the industry. Pharmaceutical sales representatives should be aware of these factors and present their offerings in a way that demonstrates potential financial and professional benefits, thereby appealing to these external motivators.

Building rapport with healthcare professionals involves understanding their unique motivations and addressing them effectively. By engaging in active listening, sales representatives can uncover the specific needs and goals of their healthcare counterparts. This rapport can lead to more productive negotiations, as healthcare professionals feel valued and understood. Furthermore, demonstrating empathy and a genuine interest in their challenges can foster trust, making it easier to discuss potential solutions that align with their motivations and objectives.

Conflict resolution strategies are also impacted by these key motivators. When disagreements arise during negotiations, understanding what drives healthcare professionals can help sales reps navigate these conflicts more effectively. By acknowledging the underlying motivations behind a healthcare professional's position, sales representatives can engage in more constructive discussions, focusing on shared goals rather than opposing viewpoints. This collaborative approach not only resolves conflicts but also strengthens relationships, paving the way for future interactions and negotiations.

In conclusion, recognizing and addressing the key motivators of healthcare professionals is crucial for successful negotiations in the pharmaceutical sales environment. By connecting with their intrinsic and extrinsic motivations, building rapport, and effectively managing conflicts, pharmaceutical sales representatives can enhance their negotiation strategies. This understanding not only leads to improved sales outcomes but also promotes a collaborative environment where healthcare professionals feel supported and valued in their efforts to provide the best care for their patients.

Aligning Your Objectives with Their Needs

When negotiating in the pharmaceutical sales environment, aligning your objectives with the needs of healthcare professionals is crucial for achieving success. This alignment begins with a comprehensive understanding of the motivations and challenges faced by doctors and pharmacists. By identifying their primary goals, such as improving patient outcomes and managing costs, you can tailor your negotiation strategies to resonate with their interests. This approach not only enhances your credibility but also fosters a collaborative atmosphere, making it easier to reach mutually beneficial agreements.

Building rapport with healthcare professionals is an essential step in ensuring that your objectives align with theirs. Establishing trust allows for open communication, where both parties can express their needs and concerns. As a pharmaceutical sales representative, you should focus on active listening and empathy, which are vital components of effective communication. By demonstrating genuine interest in their perspectives, you create an environment where healthcare professionals feel valued and understood, paving the way for more productive negotiations.

Data-driven negotiation tactics can significantly enhance the alignment of your objectives with the needs of healthcare providers. Utilizing relevant data and analytics allows you to present compelling evidence that supports your proposals. Whether it's showcasing how your product can improve patient outcomes or how it delivers cost savings, data can bridge the gap between your goals and the needs of doctors and pharmacists. This approach not only substantiates your claims but also empowers healthcare professionals to make informed decisions based on solid evidence.

Conflict is an inevitable aspect of negotiations, particularly in the high-stakes environment of pharmaceutical sales. When disagreements arise, employing conflict resolution strategies becomes essential. Understanding the root causes of the conflict and addressing them collaboratively can help realign your objectives with the needs of the other party. By focusing on solutions rather than problems, you can transform potential roadblocks into opportunities for deeper collaboration and understanding.

Lastly, leveraging technology can enhance the process of aligning your objectives with the needs of healthcare professionals. Tools such as CRM systems and communication platforms enable you to track interactions, gather insights, and analyze trends in real-time. This technological support can help you identify patterns in healthcare providers' preferences and needs, allowing you to adjust your negotiation tactics accordingly. By integrating technology into your approach, you not only streamline your negotiation process but also ensure that your objectives remain closely aligned with the evolving requirements of doctors and pharmacists.

The Role of Incentives in Negotiations

Incentives play a pivotal role in negotiations within the pharmaceutical industry, influencing the outcomes not only in terms of sales but also in fostering long-term relationships with healthcare professionals. For pharmaceutical sales representatives, understanding the different types of incentives—monetary and non-monetary—that can be effectively employed is crucial. Monetary incentives may include discounts, rebates, or promotional offers, while non-monetary incentives might consist of providing valuable information, educational resources, or support for continuing medical education. Recognizing the unique motivations of doctors and pharmacists allows sales reps to tailor their incentive strategies, making negotiations more compelling and aligned with the interests of their counterparts.

Effective negotiation requires a deep understanding of the healthcare professionals' motivations and needs. Doctors, for instance, may prioritize patient outcomes and the efficacy of treatments over financial incentives. Therefore, presenting data-driven insights that demonstrate how a product improves patient care can serve as a powerful incentive. Similarly, pharmacists may be motivated by factors such as ease of dispensing, product availability, and patient satisfaction. When sales representatives leverage these insights, they can create incentives that resonate with the specific motivations of healthcare professionals, enhancing the likelihood of successful negotiations.

Building rapport with healthcare professionals is essential for successful negotiations, and incentives can significantly aid this process. When sales reps offer value that extends beyond mere transactions—such as educational workshops or support for patient education—the relationship evolves into a partnership. This approach fosters trust and loyalty, which are vital for long-term success in pharmaceutical sales. By aligning incentives with the goals and challenges faced by healthcare professionals, sales representatives position themselves as allies rather than just vendors, facilitating more open and productive negotiations.

Conflict resolution strategies are often intertwined with the use of incentives in negotiations. When disagreements arise, having established a foundation of goodwill through effective incentives can serve as a buffer. For example, if a pharmacist feels undervalued due to pricing disputes, a well-timed non-monetary incentive, such as access to exclusive training or resources, can help de-escalate tensions. This method not only addresses the immediate conflict but also reinforces the value of the sales representative's offerings, paving the way for future negotiations.

Ultimately, ethical considerations must guide the use of incentives in pharmaceutical negotiations. Sales representatives are tasked with balancing the line between persuasive tactics and ethical practices. Transparency in how incentives are presented and the motivations behind them is crucial to maintaining integrity in negotiations. When incentives are framed in a way that prioritizes patient welfare and ethical standards, it enhances the credibility of the sales representative and the company they represent. This approach not only ensures compliance with industry regulations but also solidifies the foundation for sustainable relationships with healthcare professionals.

Chapter 8: Team Collaboration Strategies in Pharmaceutical Sales

Building a Cohesive Team

Building a cohesive team is fundamental for pharmaceutical sales representatives aiming to master the art of negotiation. A well-functioning team not only enhances individual performance but also significantly improves overall sales outcomes. Collaboration among team members fosters a culture of support, where insights and strategies can be shared freely. This synergy is particularly important in navigating the complexities of healthcare relationships, allowing the team to present a unified front to doctors and pharmacists. By recognizing the strengths and weaknesses of each team member, pharmaceutical sales reps can leverage collective knowledge to enhance their negotiation tactics.

Effective communication is the cornerstone of a cohesive team. Sales representatives must establish open lines of communication to discuss strategies, share experiences, and provide feedback. Regular team meetings can serve as a platform for discussing successes and challenges faced in the field. By encouraging an environment where team members feel comfortable sharing their perspectives, everyone can learn from each other's experiences. This approach not only builds rapport among team members but also allows for the development of more effective negotiation techniques tailored to the unique needs of healthcare professionals.

Understanding the motivations of doctors and pharmacists is another critical aspect of building a cohesive team. Each team member should be equipped with knowledge about the specific needs and concerns of healthcare professionals they engage with. By aligning their collective efforts towards understanding these motivations, the team can create more compelling value propositions. This alignment fosters a sense of purpose within the team, as members work together toward a common goal of delivering exceptional service to their clients while achieving sales targets. A unified understanding of client motivations enhances the team's ability to negotiate effectively.

Conflict resolution strategies are essential for maintaining harmony within a cohesive team. In the fast-paced environment of pharmaceutical sales, disagreements can arise, whether they pertain to sales tactics or individual performance. Teams should establish clear protocols for addressing conflicts constructively. Encouraging a culture that views conflict as an opportunity for growth can help mitigate negative outcomes. When conflicts are resolved amicably, it strengthens relationships among team members and reinforces a commitment to collective success. This approach not only improves team morale but also enhances the team's overall effectiveness in negotiations.

Lastly, leveraging technology can significantly contribute to building a cohesive team. In the pharmaceutical industry, data-driven negotiation tactics are essential for remaining competitive. Utilizing tools such as customer relationship management (CRM) systems and data analytics can provide valuable insights into customer preferences and market trends. By sharing these insights within the team, members can align their strategies and enhance their negotiation approaches. Embracing technology facilitates collaboration and ensures that all team members are informed and prepared, ultimately leading to more successful negotiations with healthcare professionals. A cohesive team equipped with the right tools and strategies can navigate the complexities of pharmaceutical sales with confidence and effectiveness.

Sharing Knowledge and Best Practices

Sharing knowledge and best practices is essential for pharmaceutical sales representatives who aim to excel in negotiations with healthcare professionals. The dynamic nature of the pharmaceutical industry necessitates that sales reps stay informed about not only their products but also the evolving needs and motivations of doctors, pharmacists, and their own teammates. By fostering a culture of knowledge sharing, representatives can enhance their negotiation skills, build rapport with healthcare professionals, and create a more cohesive team environment. This subchapter will discuss the importance of sharing knowledge, outline effective strategies, and highlight the role of collaboration in achieving negotiation success.

One effective way to share knowledge is through regular team meetings and training sessions. These gatherings provide an opportunity for sales representatives to discuss recent experiences, share insights from interactions with healthcare professionals, and analyze outcomes of various negotiation tactics. Encouraging team members to present case studies or role-playing scenarios can facilitate deeper understanding and enable reps to draw lessons from both successes and challenges. This collaborative approach not only enhances individual skills but also strengthens team dynamics, leading to improved performance in the field.

Utilizing technology can significantly enhance the process of knowledge sharing among pharmaceutical sales teams. Digital platforms, such as collaborative software and communication tools, enable representatives to share resources, strategies, and updates in real time. Creating a centralized database of best practices, negotiation techniques, and case studies allows team members to access valuable information at their convenience. Furthermore, webinars and online training modules can be employed to reach geographically dispersed teams, ensuring that all sales reps have access to the same high-quality training and knowledge regardless of location.

In addition to internal sharing, engaging with external networks can provide pharmaceutical sales representatives with fresh perspectives and innovative strategies. Participating in industry conferences, workshops, and online forums allows reps to connect with peers and experts from different organizations. These interactions can lead to the sharing of successful negotiation techniques and insights into various healthcare markets. By staying connected to the broader pharmaceutical community, sales representatives can adapt their strategies based on industry trends and emerging best practices.

The ethical considerations in pharmaceutical negotiations also play a crucial role in knowledge sharing. Representatives must be aware of the importance of maintaining integrity and transparency in their dealings with healthcare professionals. Sharing knowledge about ethical negotiation practices not only helps reps navigate complex situations but also fosters trust and credibility. By prioritizing ethical standards, sales representatives can build long-lasting relationships with doctors and pharmacists, ultimately leading to more successful negotiations and collaborations.

Leveraging Team Strengths in Negotiations

In the competitive landscape of pharmaceutical sales, leveraging team strengths during negotiations can be a game changer. Each team member brings unique skills, insights, and experiences that can enhance the negotiation process. Recognizing and utilizing these strengths not only improves the likelihood of achieving favorable outcomes but also fosters a collaborative environment where ideas and strategies can flourish. By understanding individual competencies and aligning them with negotiation goals, pharmaceutical sales representatives can present a united front that resonates with healthcare professionals.

Effective communication is crucial in negotiations, and each member of a sales team can contribute to this aspect. For instance, one team member might excel in establishing rapport with doctors, while another may possess in-depth knowledge of product details. By strategically assigning roles based on these strengths, the team can ensure that all aspects of the negotiation are covered. This specialization allows for a more thorough understanding of the healthcare professional's motivations and concerns, which can be addressed more effectively during discussions. Moreover, this approach encourages active participation and investment from all team members, enhancing overall performance.

Conflict resolution is another essential component of negotiations in pharmaceutical sales. Disagreements can arise, whether due to differing opinions on strategy or misunderstandings about product information. By leveraging the unique strengths of team members, conflict can be managed more efficiently. For example, if a disagreement occurs, a team member skilled in mediation can step in to facilitate dialogue, helping to clarify misunderstandings and find common ground. This not only resolves issues swiftly but also reinforces the collaborative spirit of the team, demonstrating to healthcare professionals that the team is cohesive and focused on mutual goals.

Data-driven negotiation tactics are increasingly important in pharmaceutical sales. Teams can harness the analytical strengths of members who excel in data interpretation to inform their strategies. By presenting evidence-based insights about market trends, patient outcomes, or product efficacy, the team can bolster their case during negotiations. Additionally, leveraging technology to share real-time data during discussions can enhance credibility and promote informed decision-making. When team members collaborate to present a unified, data-backed approach, they not only enhance their persuasive power but also build trust with healthcare professionals.

Finally, ethical considerations should always underpin negotiations in the pharmaceutical sector. Teams should leverage their collective strengths to uphold ethical standards consistently. This means fostering an environment where team members feel comfortable discussing ethical dilemmas and supporting one another in making principled decisions. By openly addressing these concerns, the team can reinforce its commitment to ethical practices, which is critical in building long-term relationships with doctors and pharmacists.

Ultimately, by effectively leveraging their strengths, pharmaceutical sales representatives can enhance their negotiation success while maintaining the integrity of their professional relationships.

Chapter 9: Data-Driven Negotiation Tactics for Pharma Reps

Utilizing Market Research

Utilizing market research is a fundamental strategy for pharmaceutical sales representatives aiming to enhance their negotiation skills. By understanding the dynamics of the pharmaceutical market, sales reps can identify trends, preferences, and behaviors that inform their approach to interacting with healthcare professionals. This knowledge enables reps to tailor their pitches effectively, ensuring that the solutions they offer align closely with the needs and motivations of doctors and pharmacists. Market research provides insights into competitor offerings, market gaps, and emerging therapeutic areas, all of which can be leveraged to establish credibility and authority during negotiations.

Effective negotiation in pharmaceutical sales requires a deep understanding of the healthcare landscape. Market research can unveil critical information about patient demographics, treatment protocols, and prescribing habits. By analyzing this data, sales representatives can better comprehend the challenges faced by healthcare providers. This understanding not only aids in building rapport but also positions the sales rep as a knowledgeable partner rather than just a vendor. When healthcare professionals see that a rep has taken the time to understand their unique environment, they are more likely to engage in meaningful discussions, paving the way for successful negotiations.

In addition to understanding healthcare professionals, utilizing market research helps sales reps to identify and articulate their value propositions clearly. A data-driven approach can reveal how a pharmaceutical product addresses specific pain points within the healthcare system, such as cost-effectiveness, improved patient outcomes, or streamlined treatment protocols. By presenting this information in a compelling manner, reps can enhance their negotiation positions. The ability to back claims with solid evidence not only builds trust but also strengthens the overall argument during negotiations, making it easier to overcome objections and secure agreements.

Furthermore, market research can play a crucial role in conflict resolution strategies. By being informed about market trends and competitor actions, sales reps can anticipate potential conflicts that may arise during negotiations. A well-prepared rep can navigate these situations more adeptly by addressing concerns with factual data and alternative solutions. This proactive approach not only minimizes conflict but also demonstrates a commitment to collaboration and partnership, essential qualities in fostering long-term relationships with healthcare professionals.

Finally, incorporating technology into the market research process can significantly enhance a sales rep's effectiveness. Utilizing tools such as CRM systems, data analytics, and digital surveys can streamline the collection of valuable market insights. By leveraging these technologies, pharmaceutical sales representatives can stay updated on market changes, customer preferences, and emerging challenges. This real-time access to information allows for agile negotiation tactics, ensuring that reps are always prepared to address the evolving needs of healthcare providers. In summary, harnessing market research is an indispensable component of negotiation mastery in pharmaceutical sales, leading to more informed decisions and successful outcomes.

Analyzing Sales Data for Insights

Analyzing sales data is a fundamental aspect of understanding market dynamics and enhancing negotiation strategies within the pharmaceutical sales landscape. For pharmaceutical sales representatives, the ability to interpret sales data effectively can lead to improved insights about customer preferences, product performance, and market trends. By examining these metrics, sales reps can identify which products resonate most with healthcare professionals and adjust their negotiation tactics accordingly.

This data-driven approach not only enhances the representative's credibility but also fosters stronger relationships with doctors and pharmacists, who appreciate a thorough understanding of the products being discussed.

In the realm of pharmaceutical sales, sales data encompasses a variety of metrics, including prescription volumes, market share, and competitive positioning. By closely monitoring these figures, representatives can discern patterns that indicate which products are gaining traction and which may require additional support or re-strategizing. For example, a significant increase in prescriptions for a particular medication may suggest that physicians are responding positively to recent promotional efforts or clinical data. Conversely, if sales are declining, it may prompt a closer examination of the factors at play, such as changes in competitor offerings or shifts in physician preferences. This analysis allows sales representatives to tailor their negotiations with informed insights.

Understanding the motivations of healthcare professionals is crucial in negotiations, and sales data can provide valuable context in this regard. By analyzing data related to prescribing habits and patient demographics, representatives can uncover insights into what drives healthcare providers' decisions. For instance, if data reveals that a doctor frequently prescribes medications for a certain demographic, a sales rep can focus their negotiation on how their product meets the specific needs of that group.

This targeted approach not only enhances the relevance of the conversation but also positions the representative as a knowledgeable partner in the healthcare provider's practice.

Furthermore, leveraging sales data fosters collaboration among team members, enhancing overall performance. When representatives share insights derived from data analysis, they contribute to a collective understanding of the market landscape. This shared knowledge can lead to more cohesive strategies when approaching healthcare professionals, allowing for unified messaging and support.

Additionally, understanding team performance metrics can help identify areas where training or support is needed, ensuring that all representatives are equipped with the tools necessary to succeed in their negotiations.

Lastly, ethical considerations must be at the forefront of data analysis practices. While leveraging sales data can be incredibly beneficial, it is essential to ensure that this information is used responsibly and transparently. Pharmaceutical sales representatives must be cautious not to manipulate data to mislead healthcare professionals. Instead, the focus should be on providing accurate information that supports informed decision-making. By maintaining high ethical standards in data utilization, representatives can build trust with healthcare professionals, which is invaluable for successful negotiations and long-term partnerships.

Making Data Work for You

Data plays a pivotal role in the negotiation landscape for pharmaceutical sales representatives. By harnessing and analyzing data, sales reps can enhance their strategies, making informed decisions that resonate with healthcare professionals. Understanding the nuances of data, including sales statistics, market trends, and customer feedback, empowers representatives to tailor their approach to meet the specific needs and motivations of doctors and pharmacists. This customization not only increases the likelihood of successful negotiations but also fosters stronger relationships built on trust and relevance.

To effectively utilize data in negotiations, sales representatives must first identify the key metrics that drive their success. This includes understanding the prescribing habits of doctors, the inventory turnover rates of pharmacies, and the feedback from healthcare providers regarding product efficacy. By compiling and analyzing this data, representatives can identify patterns and trends that inform their negotiation strategy. For instance, if data reveals that a particular medication is highly prescribed in a specific region, reps can focus their discussions on the benefits of that medication, addressing any concerns that healthcare professionals may have based on their previous experiences.

Furthermore, sales reps should leverage data to preemptively counter objections that may arise during negotiations. By anticipating the needs and concerns of healthcare professionals, reps can present data that supports their proposals and demonstrates the value of their products. For example, if a doctor expresses hesitation about a new medication due to side effects, having clinical trial data readily available can help alleviate those concerns. This data-driven approach not only strengthens the sales pitch but also showcases the representative's commitment to transparency and ethical considerations, which are crucial in building rapport with healthcare professionals.

In addition to using data during negotiations, sales representatives should also collaborate with their teammates to share insights and strategies derived from data analysis. Team collaboration can lead to a more comprehensive understanding of the market landscape and enable representatives to develop a unified approach to negotiations. Regular meetings to discuss data findings, share success stories, and refine strategies can enhance overall team performance. By collectively analyzing data, reps can ensure that their messaging is consistent and resonates effectively with their target audience.

Finally, embracing technology can further amplify the effectiveness of data utilization in negotiations. Numerous tools are available that allow pharmaceutical sales representatives to collect, analyze, and present data in compelling ways. Utilizing Customer Relationship Management (CRM) systems can streamline the process of tracking interactions with healthcare professionals and analyzing the outcomes of previous negotiations. By integrating technology into their negotiation tactics, representatives not only optimize their efficiency but also position themselves as informed and resourceful partners in the eyes of doctors and pharmacists.

This technological edge, combined with a data-driven mindset, ultimately leads to more successful negotiations and lasting professional relationships.

Chapter 10: Ethical Considerations in Pharmaceutical Negotiations

Understanding Regulatory Compliance

Understanding regulatory compliance is crucial for pharmaceutical sales representatives as it directly impacts the negotiation process with healthcare professionals. Regulatory compliance refers to the adherence to laws, guidelines, and specifications relevant to the pharmaceutical industry. This encompasses a wide range of regulations, including those set forth by the Food and Drug Administration (FDA), the Drug Enforcement Administration (DEA), and various state and federal laws.

Understanding these regulations is essential not just for legal compliance but also for establishing trust and credibility with doctors, pharmacists, and colleagues.

Pharmaceutical sales representatives must be well-versed in the regulations that govern their interactions with healthcare professionals. This includes knowing what information can be shared, how to present data, and the limitations on promotional activities. For instance, the FDA has strict guidelines on how pharmaceutical products can be advertised and the claims that can be made. Being knowledgeable about these regulations allows sales reps to avoid potential pitfalls during negotiations and to engage in ethical discussions that prioritize the needs and concerns of healthcare professionals.

Moreover, compliance plays a vital role in the negotiation dynamics with healthcare professionals. Doctors and pharmacists are increasingly aware of compliance issues and may have concerns about the information presented to them. By demonstrating a solid understanding of regulatory compliance, sales representatives can build rapport and foster a collaborative environment. This not only helps in negotiating better terms but also positions the sales rep as a reliable partner who respects the ethical boundaries of the pharmaceutical industry.

Additionally, effective communication skills are intertwined with regulatory compliance. Pharmaceutical sales reps must be adept at conveying complex information in a manner that is both clear and compliant with regulations. This requires a delicate balance of assertiveness and respect for the healthcare professional's expertise and autonomy. By practicing effective communication techniques, reps can ensure that their proposals are well-received and that they maintain a professional demeanor during negotiations, even when faced with resistance or skepticism.

Finally, the ability to navigate compliance issues can significantly enhance conflict resolution strategies in pharmaceutical sales. When disputes arise, whether regarding product information or promotional practices, having a thorough understanding of regulatory guidelines equips sales representatives with the necessary tools to address these conflicts constructively. By focusing on compliance, sales reps can help facilitate discussions that lead to mutually beneficial outcomes, thereby reinforcing their role as trusted advisors in the healthcare ecosystem.

Ethical Dilemmas in Sales

Ethical dilemmas in sales present significant challenges for pharmaceutical sales representatives, who must navigate the complex landscape of healthcare while maintaining integrity and professionalism. As representatives engage with healthcare professionals, they often find themselves balancing the needs of their companies with the ethical responsibility to provide accurate information and prioritize patient care. This delicate balance is crucial, as the choices made during negotiations can impact not only business relationships but also patient outcomes and the overall reputation of the pharmaceutical industry.

One prevalent ethical dilemma involves the pressure to meet sales targets while ensuring that the information provided to healthcare professionals is truthful and complete. Representatives may feel compelled to emphasize the benefits of their products while downplaying potential risks or side effects. This practice can lead to mistrust among healthcare providers and ultimately may compromise patient safety. It is essential for pharmaceutical sales reps to recognize that transparency and honesty are fundamental to building long-term relationships with doctors and pharmacists, which can ultimately lead to better sales outcomes.

Another ethical concern arises when sales representatives face requests for gifts or incentives from healthcare providers. While offering educational materials or sponsoring events can be acceptable, the line can quickly blur when it comes to personal gifts or excessive incentives. Such practices can create conflicts of interest and raise questions about the integrity of the representative's intentions. Pharmaceutical sales reps must navigate these requests carefully, adhering to company policies and industry regulations, while finding ways to engage healthcare professionals that do not compromise ethical standards.

Additionally, the use of data in negotiations poses its own set of ethical challenges. Representatives often leverage data to demonstrate the efficacy of their products, but the interpretation and presentation of this data must be done with care. Misleading statistics or selective reporting can distort the truth and misinform healthcare providers. It is critical for sales reps to ensure that they are using data responsibly and ethically, providing a complete view of the information that allows healthcare professionals to make informed decisions for their patients.

Lastly, ethical dilemmas in sales necessitate a strong commitment to collaboration and communication within the sales team. When faced with challenging situations, representatives should feel empowered to discuss their concerns with colleagues and seek guidance. Establishing an open dialogue about ethical practices not only strengthens the team's integrity but also fosters a culture of accountability. By sharing experiences and strategies for ethical decision-making, pharmaceutical sales reps can enhance their negotiation skills while ensuring that their actions align with the fundamental values of professionalism and respect for patient welfare.

Building a Reputation for Integrity

Building a reputation for integrity is essential for pharmaceutical sales representatives as it lays the foundation for successful negotiations and long-term relationships with healthcare professionals. Integrity fosters trust, which is paramount in the pharmaceutical industry, where healthcare providers seek reliable partners in their decision-making processes. Sales representatives who consistently demonstrate ethical behavior, honesty, and transparency in their dealings will find that these attributes enhance their credibility.

This credibility not only improves negotiations with doctors and pharmacists but also encourages a collaborative atmosphere among coworkers, reinforcing a unified approach to sales.

To build a reputation for integrity, pharmaceutical sales representatives must prioritize effective communication. This involves not only conveying information clearly but also listening actively to understand the needs and motivations of healthcare professionals. By engaging in open dialogue, sales reps can align their offerings with the specific goals of doctors and pharmacists, demonstrating that they value their perspectives.

Moreover, by sharing relevant data and evidence-based information, reps can position themselves as knowledgeable partners who prioritize the best interests of their clients and patients alike.

Conflict resolution is another critical aspect of building integrity. Disagreements may arise in negotiations, but how they are handled can significantly impact a sales representative's reputation. Approaching conflicts with a mindset focused on collaboration rather than confrontation allows for constructive discussions. Sales reps should strive to find mutually beneficial solutions, emphasizing a commitment to ethical practices and the long-term well-being of patients. When healthcare professionals see representatives navigating challenges with integrity, it reinforces the belief that they can be trusted in future interactions.

Team collaboration is also vital in fostering an environment of integrity. When sales representatives work cohesively with their colleagues, it creates a unified front that reflects shared values and goals. This teamwork not only improves internal communication but also translates to more consistent messaging in the field. By encouraging open discussions about ethical dilemmas and negotiation strategies, teams can establish a culture of integrity that permeates their interactions with healthcare professionals. A strong, collaborative team can amplify the individual reputations of its members, making integrity a collective asset.

Finally, leveraging technology can enhance the ability of pharmaceutical sales representatives to uphold a reputation for integrity. Digital tools can facilitate data-driven negotiations, providing sales reps with valuable insights into market trends and healthcare provider preferences. By utilizing technology to present accurate and relevant information, representatives can reinforce their commitment to transparency. Additionally, technology can enable better communication and collaboration among team members, ensuring that everyone is aligned in their approach to negotiations. Ultimately, a strong reputation for integrity not only leads to successful sales outcomes but also fosters a positive impact on patient care and the broader healthcare community.

Chapter 11: Role-Playing Scenarios for Sales Training

Designing Effective Role-Playing Exercises

Designing effective role-playing exercises is essential for pharmaceutical sales representatives seeking to enhance their negotiation skills. These exercises should be carefully structured to reflect real-world scenarios that sales professionals encounter when interacting with healthcare providers. By creating authentic situations that mimic the complexities of pharmaceutical negotiations, sales reps can practice their communication strategies, build rapport, and develop conflict resolution techniques in a safe and controlled environment.

To begin, it is crucial to identify the key objectives of the role-playing exercises. Each session should have a clear focus, whether it is mastering negotiation techniques, understanding the motivations of doctors and pharmacists, or refining effective communication skills. By establishing specific goals, participants can engage more meaningfully in the exercises and assess their progress in achieving the desired outcomes. This clarity will also help trainers to provide targeted feedback that is relevant and actionable for participants.

Next, participants should be assigned roles that reflect various stakeholders involved in the negotiation process. This could include the pharmaceutical sales representative, a physician, a pharmacist, or even a colleague who acts as a mentor or challenger. By rotating roles, participants gain a broader perspective on the negotiation dynamics and can better understand the motivations and concerns of each party. This practice fosters empathy and strengthens the ability to build rapport, which is vital for successful negotiations in the pharmaceutical industry.

Incorporating real-life scenarios into the role-playing exercises enhances their effectiveness. Sales reps should draw from their own experiences or common challenges faced in the field. Scenarios can range from negotiating product placements in a pharmacy to addressing a doctor's hesitance about a new medication. By using realistic contexts, participants can practice applying data-driven negotiation tactics and ethical considerations, equipping them with the tools needed to navigate complex conversations with healthcare professionals.

Finally, debriefing after each role-playing session is critical for reinforcing learning. Trainers should facilitate discussions that allow participants to reflect on their performance, share insights, and identify areas for improvement. This collaborative feedback process encourages continuous learning and fosters a team-oriented environment where sales representatives can support each other's growth. By designing effective role-playing exercises that include clear objectives, realistic scenarios, and thorough debriefing, pharmaceutical sales reps can significantly enhance their negotiation mastery, leading to more fruitful interactions with doctors, pharmacists, and their colleagues.

Learning from Real-World Scenarios

Learning from real-world scenarios is essential for pharmaceutical sales representatives seeking to enhance their negotiation skills. Engaging directly with healthcare professionals provides an invaluable opportunity to observe, experience, and analyze various negotiation dynamics in practice. These scenarios often reveal the nuances of communication, the importance of reading non-verbal cues, and the impact of emotional intelligence on the negotiation process.

By reflecting on these experiences, sales reps can identify effective strategies and adapt their approaches to better align with the expectations and motivations of doctors and pharmacists.

One of the most instructive ways to learn from real-world scenarios is through role-playing exercises. These simulations allow sales representatives to practice negotiating in a controlled environment while receiving immediate feedback from peers and mentors. By recreating various situations, such as discussing product benefits with a skeptical doctor or addressing a pharmacist's concerns about medication availability, reps can experiment with different techniques and strategies.

This hands-on approach not only builds confidence but also enhances the ability to think on one's feet during actual negotiations.

Another critical aspect of learning from real-world scenarios is understanding the motivations of healthcare professionals. Observing interactions with doctors and pharmacists allows sales representatives to gain insights into what drives decision-making in these roles. For instance, recognizing that a pharmacist prioritizes patient safety and cost-effectiveness can inform how a rep presents a product's value proposition. By tailoring their message to meet the specific needs and concerns of their audience, reps can foster stronger relationships and increase the likelihood of successful negotiations.

Additionally, conflict resolution is a vital skill that can be honed through real-world experiences. Learning to navigate disagreements or misunderstandings with healthcare professionals requires patience, empathy, and effective communication skills. By reflecting on past encounters where conflicts arose, sales representatives can analyze their responses and identify areas for improvement. This self-assessment not only aids in personal growth but also equips reps with the tools to manage future disputes more effectively, ultimately leading to more productive outcomes.

Finally, leveraging technology and data in negotiations presents another avenue for learning from real-world scenarios. Utilizing digital tools to gather and analyze market data can inform negotiation strategies, making them more data-driven and persuasive. By observing how successful colleagues use technology to enhance their negotiations, sales representatives can adopt similar practices to improve their own effectiveness. This integration of technology not only streamlines communication but also reinforces the importance of being well-prepared, which is crucial in the competitive pharmaceutical landscape.

Feedback and Improvement Techniques

Feedback plays a crucial role in the continuous development of pharmaceutical sales representatives, particularly when it comes to negotiating with healthcare professionals. Effective feedback mechanisms enable sales reps to assess their performance, understand areas for improvement, and refine their negotiation strategies. Regularly soliciting feedback from peers, managers, and even clients can provide valuable insights into what works and what doesn't.

This process also fosters a culture of openness and collaboration, essential for building strong relationships within teams and with healthcare professionals.

One effective technique for gathering feedback is the use of structured debriefing sessions after important sales calls or negotiations. These sessions allow sales representatives to reflect on their experiences, share successes, and discuss challenges encountered during the negotiation process. By analyzing these situations in a group setting, team members can offer different perspectives and suggest alternative approaches that may not have been considered initially. This collaborative effort can enhance individual skill sets and improve overall team performance in negotiations.

Moreover, leveraging technology to facilitate feedback can streamline the process and make it more efficient. Tools such as customer relationship management (CRM) systems can track interactions with healthcare professionals, allowing sales reps to review data on previous negotiations and identify patterns or trends.

Additionally, digital platforms can enable real-time feedback from team members, ensuring that insights are captured promptly and applied effectively. Embracing technology not only improves the feedback loop but also supports a data-driven approach to refining negotiation tactics.

Incorporating role-playing scenarios into training sessions is another beneficial technique for improving negotiation skills based on feedback. By simulating real-life negotiation situations, sales reps can practice their techniques in a low-stakes environment. Feedback from trainers and peers during these sessions can highlight strengths and weaknesses, guiding individuals on how to adapt their strategies.

This hands-on approach not only builds confidence but also prepares sales representatives to handle complex negotiations with healthcare professionals more effectively.

Finally, it is essential to establish a mindset focused on continuous improvement. Sales representatives should view feedback not as criticism but as an opportunity for growth. Embracing an attitude of lifelong learning encourages reps to remain adaptable and responsive to the evolving landscape of pharmaceutical sales. By actively seeking and implementing feedback, pharmaceutical sales representatives can enhance their negotiation techniques, ultimately leading to better outcomes in their interactions with doctors, pharmacists, and team members.

Chapter 12: Leveraging Technology in Pharmaceutical Negotiations

Tools and Platforms for Negotiation

In the realm of pharmaceutical sales, effective negotiation requires not only skill and strategy but also the right tools and platforms to facilitate successful outcomes. The digital transformation in the industry has opened up various avenues for sales representatives to enhance their negotiation capabilities. Familiarity with these tools can empower sales reps to engage more effectively with healthcare professionals, streamline communication, and ultimately close more deals. Leveraging technology in this context allows for a more data-driven approach, making negotiations not just intuitive but also strategically informed.

One crucial platform for pharmaceutical sales representatives is Customer Relationship Management (CRM) software. These systems enable sales reps to manage interactions with doctors and pharmacists efficiently. A well-implemented CRM provides insights into customer preferences, previous interactions, and purchasing behavior, allowing sales reps to tailor their negotiation strategies accordingly.

By having access to comprehensive data, sales representatives can identify key motivations of their healthcare clients, which can be pivotal in crafting persuasive arguments during negotiations.

In addition to CRM tools, communication platforms such as video conferencing software have become invaluable in the negotiation process. These platforms allow for face-to-face interactions even when in-person meetings are not feasible. Such tools facilitate the building of rapport with healthcare professionals, as they enable a more personal connection than traditional email or phone communication. Moreover, video conferencing can enhance clarity during discussions, allowing for real-time feedback and the ability to share visual data or presentations that can strengthen the sales narrative.

Collaboration tools are equally essential in fostering teamwork among pharmaceutical sales representatives. Platforms that support project management and communication, such as Slack or Microsoft Teams, enable sales teams to share insights, strategies, and updates in real-time. This collective knowledge can be leveraged during negotiations, as teammates can contribute their experiences and knowledge about specific healthcare providers or market trends. Such collaboration not only enhances individual performance but also creates a unified approach to negotiation that can be more effective in reaching desired outcomes.

Lastly, role-playing scenarios facilitated by training platforms can significantly enhance negotiation skills for pharmaceutical sales reps. These simulations provide a safe environment for sales representatives to practice their techniques, receive feedback, and refine their strategies before engaging with real clients. Incorporating ethical considerations and conflict resolution strategies into these exercises ensures that reps are not only prepared to negotiate effectively but also to handle challenging situations with integrity. Ultimately, the combination of these tools and platforms equips pharmaceutical sales representatives with the resources they need to master negotiations with healthcare professionals, leading to greater success in their sales endeavors.

The Role of CRM Systems

The role of Customer Relationship Management (CRM) systems in pharmaceutical sales is pivotal for enhancing negotiation strategies and fostering successful interactions with healthcare professionals. CRM systems serve as comprehensive databases that enable sales representatives to track and analyze customer interactions, preferences, and behaviors. This data-driven approach allows pharmaceutical sales reps to tailor their communication and negotiation tactics to meet the specific needs of doctors and pharmacists. By leveraging CRM systems, sales representatives can ensure that their discussions are relevant and focused, significantly improving their chances of closing deals and building long-term relationships.

Effective CRM systems also facilitate the segmentation of healthcare professionals based on various criteria, such as prescribing habits, specialty, and previous interactions. This segmentation empowers sales reps to develop targeted strategies that resonate with each segment's unique motivations and concerns. Understanding these nuances is crucial in the pharmaceutical industry, where practitioners may have varying degrees of openness to new products or services.

By utilizing CRM data to inform their negotiation techniques, sales representatives can engage more meaningfully with healthcare professionals, thereby increasing the likelihood of successful outcomes.

Moreover, CRM systems provide valuable insights into the performance of sales strategies over time. By analyzing historical data, sales representatives can identify which negotiation tactics have been most effective in different scenarios. This continuous feedback loop allows for the refinement of negotiation techniques, ensuring that representatives are equipped with the most effective tools and methods to engage with healthcare professionals.

The ability to assess and adapt strategies based on empirical evidence not only enhances individual performance but also contributes to the overall success of the sales team.

Collaboration among sales team members is another significant aspect of CRM systems. These platforms facilitate the sharing of information and insights among team members, ensuring that everyone is on the same page regarding client interactions and ongoing negotiations. This collaborative environment fosters a culture of support and teamwork, essential for addressing complex negotiation scenarios that may arise in the pharmaceutical sales landscape. By working together and utilizing shared data from the CRM, sales representatives can present a unified front to healthcare professionals, enhancing their credibility and effectiveness during negotiations.

Lastly, ethical considerations in pharmaceutical negotiations are paramount, and CRM systems can help ensure that representatives adhere to these standards. By maintaining detailed records of interactions and agreements, CRM systems promote transparency and accountability in the negotiation process. This not only helps to mitigate potential conflicts but also reinforces trust with healthcare professionals, who are increasingly scrutinizing the sales practices of pharmaceutical companies.

By integrating ethical practices with data-driven strategies, sales representatives can navigate the complexities of pharmaceutical negotiations with integrity, ultimately leading to more successful outcomes for all parties involved.

Future Trends in Negotiation Technology

As the pharmaceutical landscape continues to evolve, negotiation technology is set to play a pivotal role in shaping the future of sales interactions. Emerging tools and software are designed to enhance the efficiency and effectiveness of negotiations between sales representatives and healthcare professionals. These technologies will not only streamline communication but also provide valuable insights into decision-making processes, allowing pharmaceutical sales reps to tailor their approaches to meet the specific needs of doctors and pharmacists.

By leveraging data analytics, sales representatives can anticipate objections, understand motivations, and construct compelling arguments that resonate with their audience.

Artificial intelligence (AI) is one of the most significant trends influencing negotiation technology. AI-powered platforms can analyze vast amounts of data to identify trends and patterns in healthcare decisions. This capability allows pharmaceutical sales reps to engage in more informed negotiations, as they can present data-driven evidence that supports their product's efficacy and value. Furthermore, AI tools can simulate various negotiation scenarios, enabling sales reps to practice and refine their strategies in a risk-free environment. This not only enhances their preparation but also boosts their confidence during actual negotiations.

Collaboration tools are also making a substantial impact on how pharmaceutical sales teams negotiate. With the rise of remote work and virtual meetings, effective communication has never been more critical. Platforms that facilitate real-time collaboration enable sales teams to share insights, strategize, and even role-play negotiation scenarios with ease. These tools help ensure that all team members are aligned in their messaging and approaches, which is essential when negotiating with healthcare professionals who may need to hear a consistent narrative from various representatives. By fostering a collaborative environment, sales teams can enhance their overall negotiation effectiveness.

Moreover, the integration of customer relationship management (CRM) systems with negotiation technology provides a comprehensive view of client interactions. CRMs that incorporate negotiation features allow pharmaceutical sales reps to track previous discussions, understand client preferences, and document outcomes in a systematic way. This information is invaluable for preparing for future negotiations, as it allows reps to build on past interactions and continuously improve their techniques. The ability to reference historical data during negotiations can strengthen rapport with healthcare professionals, as it demonstrates an understanding of their needs and concerns.

Finally, ethical considerations in negotiation technology must not be overlooked. As technology advances, it is crucial for pharmaceutical sales representatives to remain vigilant about maintaining ethical standards in their negotiations. Transparency and integrity should guide their use of technology, ensuring that all interactions with healthcare professionals are grounded in trust and respect. As the industry adapts to technological innovations, sales reps must balance leveraging these tools with a commitment to ethical practices that prioritize the well-being of their clients and patients.

Chapter 13: Conclusion and Next Steps

Continuing Your Negotiation Education

Continuing your education in negotiation is essential for pharmaceutical sales representatives who seek to excel in their interactions with healthcare professionals. The dynamic landscape of the pharmaceutical industry demands that sales reps not only understand their products but also master the art of negotiation.

This involves honing skills such as effective communication, building rapport, and understanding the motivations of doctors and pharmacists. Engaging in ongoing education can provide you with the latest strategies and techniques to navigate complex negotiations effectively.

One effective way to enhance your negotiation skills is through formal training programs. Many organizations offer workshops and courses specifically designed for pharmaceutical sales professionals. These programs often cover a range of topics, including conflict resolution strategies and ethical considerations in negotiations. Participating in these educational opportunities allows you to learn from industry experts, gain insights into best practices, and develop a deeper understanding of how to approach negotiations with integrity and confidence.

Another vital component of your negotiation education is the practice of role-playing scenarios. By simulating real-life negotiation situations, you can test your skills in a safe environment and receive constructive feedback from peers and trainers. Role-playing not only helps to reinforce theoretical knowledge but also provides a platform for exploring different negotiation tactics and refining your approach. This hands-on experience can significantly boost your ability to adapt to various negotiation styles and respond effectively to the unique challenges presented by different healthcare professionals.

In addition to formal training and role-playing, leveraging technology can enhance your negotiation education. Online resources, such as webinars, podcasts, and industry publications, offer valuable insights into current trends and innovative negotiation strategies. Utilizing these tools can keep you informed about the latest developments in the pharmaceutical sector and help you stay ahead of the competition. Moreover, many platforms provide opportunities for networking with fellow sales representatives, allowing you to exchange ideas and learn from each other's experiences.

Lastly, fostering a culture of continuous learning within your team can significantly impact your collective negotiation effectiveness. Encouraging open discussions about negotiation experiences and outcomes can lead to valuable lessons and shared knowledge. Collaborating with your coworkers to analyze past negotiations and strategize future approaches can create a supportive environment that enhances everyone's skills. By prioritizing ongoing education and collaboration, you can ensure that your negotiation strategies remain relevant and effective in the ever-evolving pharmaceutical industry.

Setting Personal Goals for Improvement

Setting personal goals for improvement is essential for pharmaceutical sales representatives aiming to enhance their negotiation skills and overall effectiveness. Establishing clear, measurable, and attainable goals provides a roadmap for professional development. By focusing on specific areas such as improving communication techniques, understanding the motivations of healthcare professionals, or refining conflict resolution strategies, sales reps can create a structured approach to their growth. This deliberate effort not only increases individual performance but also contributes to the success of the broader team and the organization.

To begin the process of setting personal goals, representatives should conduct a self-assessment to identify their strengths and weaknesses in negotiation scenarios. This reflection can involve analyzing past interactions with doctors, pharmacists, and colleagues to pinpoint areas for improvement. For instance, if a rep struggles to build rapport with healthcare professionals, a goal might be to develop active listening skills or tailor communication styles to better suit individual personalities. By understanding where they stand, reps can formulate targeted goals that address their specific needs and challenges.

Once representatives have identified their focus areas, they should employ the SMART criteria—Specific, Measurable, Achievable, Relevant, and Time-bound—to develop their goals. For example, rather than setting a vague goal like "improve negotiation skills," a more effective goal would be "increase the success rate of closing deals by 15% within the next quarter." This clarity ensures that progress can be tracked and adjustments can be made as necessary. Additionally, aligning personal goals with organizational objectives enhances motivation and reinforces the importance of each rep's contributions to the team's success.

Regularly revisiting and revising these goals is crucial for sustained improvement. The pharmaceutical industry is dynamic, with frequent changes in regulations, market conditions, and healthcare professional expectations. Reps should schedule periodic evaluations to review their progress, assess the relevance of their goals, and modify them in response to new challenges or opportunities. This adaptability allows sales representatives to remain agile and responsive, ensuring that their personal development remains aligned with the ever-evolving landscape of pharmaceutical sales.

Lastly, sharing goals with colleagues can foster a collaborative environment where team members support one another in achieving their objectives. Engaging in role-playing scenarios or peer feedback sessions can provide valuable insights and enhance learning experiences. By cultivating a culture of shared accountability and encouragement, sales teams can collectively elevate their negotiation prowess, resulting in improved relationships with healthcare professionals and greater success in the competitive pharmaceutical market.

Final Thoughts on Mastery in Pharmaceutical Sales Negotiations

Mastery in pharmaceutical sales negotiations requires a multifaceted approach that encompasses a range of skills and techniques. Each interaction with healthcare professionals—be it doctors, pharmacists, or colleagues—offers an opportunity to refine negotiation tactics and enhance communication. Success in this field is not merely about closing deals but rather about establishing long-term relationships built on trust and mutual benefit. As sales representatives, it is essential to recognize that every negotiation is unique, and adapting strategies to fit the context can significantly influence outcomes.

Effective communication is at the heart of successful negotiations in pharmaceuticals. Sales representatives must not only convey the value of their products but also actively listen to the needs and concerns of healthcare professionals. Understanding their motivations—whether they stem from patient care, professional development, or financial considerations—enables a sales rep to tailor their approach effectively. By asking open-ended questions and engaging in meaningful dialogue, representatives can build rapport and foster a collaborative environment where both parties feel valued.

Conflict resolution is another crucial aspect of mastering negotiations. In the pharmaceutical industry, disagreements may arise due to differing priorities or misunderstandings about product benefits. Equipping oneself with conflict resolution strategies is essential for navigating these challenges. Techniques such as empathetic listening, identifying common ground, and proposing win-win solutions can help diffuse tensions and lead to more productive discussions. These skills not only facilitate smoother negotiations but also strengthen relationships with healthcare professionals over time.

Collaboration among teammates is equally important in the negotiation process. Pharmaceutical sales often involve a team approach, particularly when dealing with complex products or large accounts. Sharing insights, strategies, and successes within a team can enhance collective knowledge and improve overall performance. Developing a culture of open communication and support among colleagues empowers sales representatives to leverage their combined strengths and tackle negotiations with greater confidence and effectiveness.

In conclusion, achieving mastery in pharmaceutical sales negotiations involves a commitment to continuous learning and adaptation. By honing communication skills, understanding the motivations of healthcare professionals, employing conflict resolution strategies, and fostering teamwork, sales representatives can enhance their negotiation capabilities. Embracing data-driven tactics and ethical considerations will further solidify their credibility and effectiveness in the field. Ultimately, the journey towards negotiation mastery is ongoing, and each experience offers valuable lessons that contribute to long-term success in pharmaceutical sales.

Enjoyed this book?

Positive reviews from awesome customers like you help others to feel confident about choosing Maples Book Solutions too.

Could you take **60 seconds** to go to Amazon platform and share your happy experiences?

We will be forever grateful. Thank you in advance for helping us out!

www.ingramcontent.com/pod-product-compliance
Lightning Source LLC
Chambersburg PA
CBHW071037240526
45469CB00006BD/2240